PUFFINS

LIVING WILD

LIVING WILD

Published by Creative Education and Creative Paperbacks
P.O. Box 227, Mankato, Minnesota 56002
Creative Education and Creative Paperbacks are imprints of The Creative Company
www.thecreativecompany.us

Design and production by Mary Herrmann
Art direction by Rita Marshall
Printed in China

Photographs by Alamy (RGR Collection), Creative Commons Wikimedia (Vernon Byrd/USFWS/Alaska Image Library, DickDaniels/carolinabirds. org, Díðrikur á Skarvanesi, Andreas Trepte/www.photo-natur.net, Matthew Zalewski), Dreamstime (Aurinko), iStockphoto (ArendTrent, KenCanning, prasit_chansareekorn, RoseMaryBush), Shutterstock (Dan Bagur, Collins93, davemhuntphotography, francesco de marco, DPS, Erni, Diane Fetzner, Attila JANDI, S.R. Maglione, Maksimilian, Ivan Marc, Martin Mecnarowski, Martin Pateman, Nick Pecker, Eugenia Petrovaskaya, Jiri Prochazka, Martin Prochazkacz, rbrown10, Olja Reven, Ron York Photography, rook 76, Gleb Tarro, Terry Tompkins, Troutnut, Warren Price Photography, Wildnerdpix)

Library of Congress Cataloging-in-Publication Data
Names: Gish, Melissa, author.
Title: Puffins / Melissa Gish.
Series: Living wild.
Includes bibliographical references and index.
Summary: A look at puffins, including their habitats, physical characteristics such as their seasonal bill plates, behaviors, relationships with humans, and their vulnerability to the changing climate today.
Identifiers: LCCN 2017038413 / ISBN 978-1-60818-959-5 (hardcover) / ISBN 978-1-62832-564-5 (pbk) / ISBN 978-1-64000-038-4 (eBook)

Subjects: LCSH: 1. Puffins—Juvenile literature. 2. Sea birds—Juvenile literature.
Classification: LCC QL696.C42 G57 2018 / DDC 598.3/3—dc23

CCSS: RI.5.1, 2, 3, 8; RST.6-8.1, 2, 5, 6, 8; RH.6-8.3, 4, 5, 6, 7, 8

First Edition HC 9 8 7 6 5 4 3 2 1
First Edition PBK 9 8 7 6 5 4 3 2 1

CREATIVE EDUCATION • CREATIVE PAPERBACKS

PUFFINS

Melissa Gish

On Machias Seal Island, off the coast of
Maine, a male Atlantic puffin challenges

a rival for territory. Perched on jagged
rocks, they eye each other aggressively.

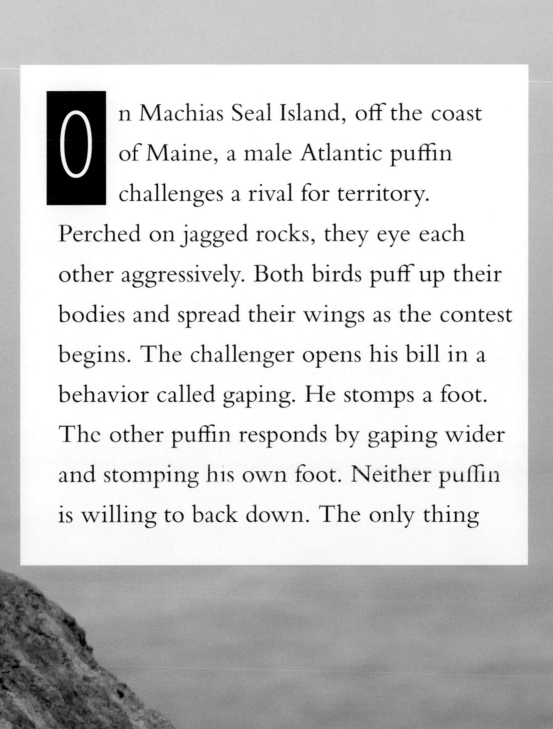

On Machias Seal Island, off the coast of Maine, a male Atlantic puffin challenges a rival for territory. Perched on jagged rocks, they eye each other aggressively. Both birds puff up their bodies and spread their wings as the contest begins. The challenger opens his bill in a behavior called gaping. He stomps a foot. The other puffin responds by gaping wider and stomping his own foot. Neither puffin is willing to back down. The only thing

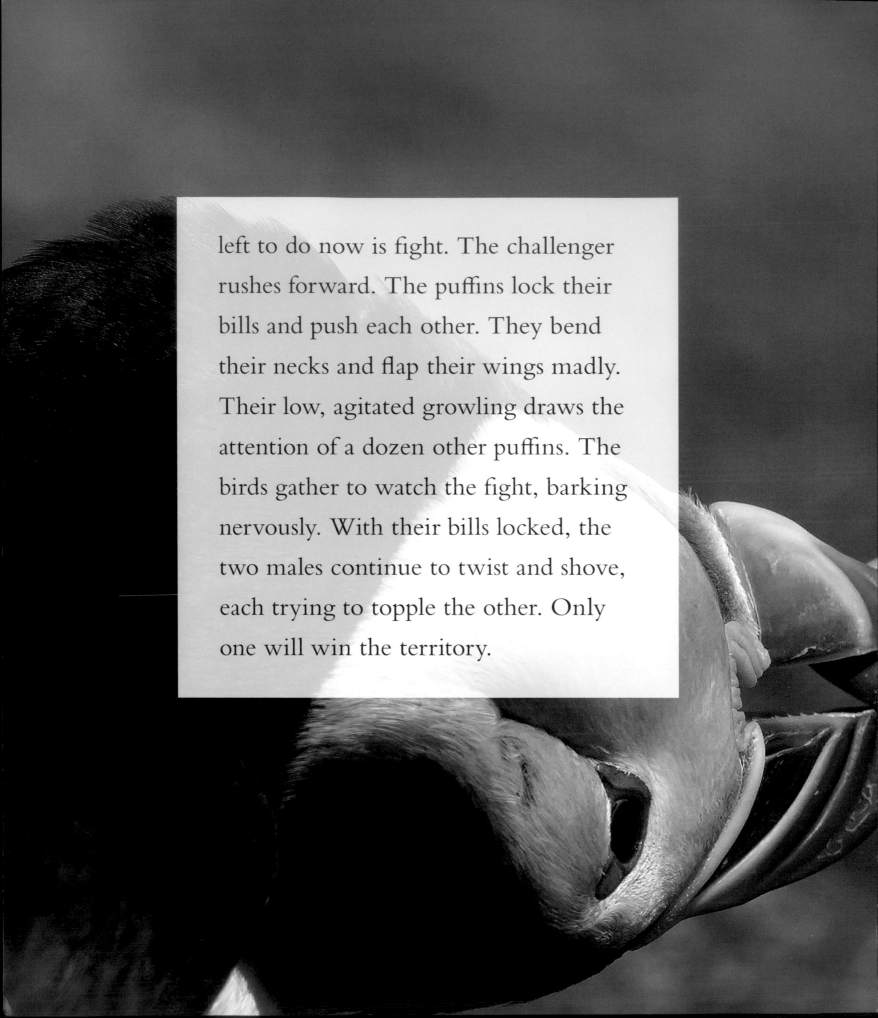

left to do now is fight. The challenger rushes forward. The puffins lock their bills and push each other. They bend their necks and flap their wings madly. Their low, agitated growling draws the attention of a dozen other puffins. The birds gather to watch the fight, barking nervously. With their bills locked, the two males continue to twist and shove, each trying to topple the other. Only one will win the territory.

WHERE IN THE WORLD THEY LIVE

■ **Atlantic Puffin**
Northern Atlantic: coastal Norway, Great Britain, Iceland, Greenland, and North America from Nunavut to Maine

■ **Horned Puffin**
Northern Pacific: coastal eastern Russia, the Aleutian Islands, and coastal Alaska and British Columbia

■ **Tufted Puffin**
Northern Pacific: coastal eastern Russia, the Aleutian Islands, and coastal North America from Alaska to northern California

Suited to cold weather, puffins spend most of their lives in and near the frigid waters of the North Atlantic and North Pacific. Mature puffins come ashore once a year to mate and nest. Once the young puffin has grown and left the burrow, its parents will return to sea until the following year. The colored squares represent the seasonal breeding grounds of each puffin species.

LITTLE BROTHERS OF THE ARCTIC

P uffins are found only in and near the North Atlantic and North Pacific oceans. They are aquatic birds that spend most of their time on the open ocean, floating on the waves or "flying" underwater. They come to shore seasonally to mate, lay eggs, and raise offspring. Then they return to the sea. What makes these small, stout birds distinctive are their large, brilliantly colored bills, which led fishermen to nickname them "sea parrots." Puffins are part of the aquatic bird family Alcidae, whose 24 living members also include auks, murrelets, guillemots, murres, auklets, and the razorbill. Atlantic, horned, and tufted puffins comprise the genus *Fratercula*, a name that comes from the Latin words *frater*, which means "brother," and *cula*, "little." This refers to not only the puffin's diminutive size but also its black, hoodlike head **plumage**, reminiscent of 16th- and 17th-century clergy ("brothers") who dressed in hooded cloaks.

During spring and summer, puffins gather on rocky shores and islands to breed and raise young. The Atlantic puffin has the largest range of the three puffin species. It nests on the coasts and islands of Great Britain, Norway,

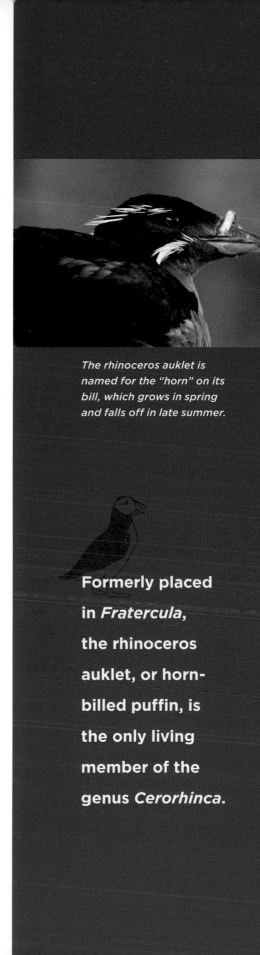

The rhinoceros auklet is named for the "horn" on its bill, which grows in spring and falls off in late summer.

Formerly placed in *Fratercula*, the rhinoceros auklet, or horn-billed puffin, is the only living member of the genus *Cerorhinca*.

Most people do not recognize puffins in winter, when their plumage and beaks are not as distinctive.

Iceland, and Greenland as well as North America from Newfoundland and Labrador to Maine. The horned puffin, named for the fleshy projections that extend above its eyes, nests on the coasts and islands of Russia's Sea of Okhotsk, Kamchatka Peninsula, and Siberia to Alaska and British Columbia. Named for the golden feather tufts on its head, the tufted puffin shares the horned puffin's range, but it travels farther south to coastal Washington, Oregon, and northern California as well as to various islands near these states.

Puffins are usually black with white faces and bellies, but their features change seasonally. During breeding season, puffins' faces are bright white, their feet and legs are brilliant orange-red, and their bills grow a striking orange covering that has bright yellow or red markings. This covering is called a bill plate. Tufted puffins lack white on their bellies, but they sport long, golden feather plumes on each side of their head. These tufts fall out before the birds return to sea for the winter. While puffins are at sea, their faces and necks turn gray, their feet and legs turn pale yellow, and their bill plates fall off, leaving their bills a dull yellowish-gray or black.

The Atlantic puffin's call has been described as sounding like a distant, buzzing chainsaw.

Sharp claws on the ends of puffins' toes help them grip rocky ledges and cliff faces as they watch for predators.

Like their ancestors, modern birds have hollow bones, making them lightweight for flight. In general, puffins weigh more in the spring (when they come to shore to breed) than they do in the fall (after expending energy to breed and raise offspring). Tufted puffins are the largest puffins. They are typically 14 to 16 inches (35.6–40.6 cm) long and weigh about 32 ounces (907 g). Their average wingspan is 29 inches (73.7 cm). Horned puffins may grow up to 15 inches (38.1 cm) long and typically weigh less than 23 ounces (652 g). Atlantic puffins are the smallest species. They average 10 inches (25.4 cm) in length with wingspans of about 23 inches (58.4 cm). In the southern part of their range, they weigh about 14 ounces (397 g), but closer to the Arctic—in northeastern Greenland and northern Norway—they can weigh up to 21 ounces (595 g).

Puffins, like all birds, are homeotherms. This means their bodies burn calories to create and conserve heat to maintain a constant temperature, no matter what the temperature is outside. Puffins live where water temperatures are between 32 and 68 °F (0 to 20 °C). They can survive in these cold habitats because their bodies are covered with two layers of feathers. Close to

Puffins can fly up to 55 miles (88.5 km) per hour, which can result in awkward landings.

Most seabirds glide on wind currents, but puffins must flap their wings up to 400 times per minute while flying.

When swimming underwater, puffins need not flap their wings as fast as when they are in the air.

The name "puffin" likely came about as an association with *puff*, referring to the fluffy appearance of puffin chicks.

the skin is a blanket of thick **down**. On top of the down are wide, waterproof feathers. Birds' feet are mostly bone, **tendon**, and scales made of **keratin**. But they are still susceptible to cold. To keep their exposed feet from freezing, puffins and their relatives have a special circulatory system. As veins carry cool blood from the feet back to the heart, the arteries carry warm blood to the feet. To keep blood in the veins from getting too cool, the arteries are entwined around the veins, heating the blood. In this way, puffins lose as little as 5 percent of their body heat through their feet.

Puffins' feet have sharp claws that are useful when digging burrows on land. The feet are webbed. This means their toes are connected by skin that spreads out and acts like a paddle, steering the puffin through the water in search of food. Unlike pelicans and gannets, which plunge into the water from great heights, puffins are surface divers. They dip their bodies underwater and "fly" by flapping their wings to pursue fish. They can travel up to three miles (4.8 km) per hour underwater. Puffins are capable of reaching depths of 230 feet (70.1 m) and spending several minutes underwater. However,

Of the three puffin species, horned puffins have the dullest-colored bills during breeding season.

Tufted puffins are the most pelagic puffin species, meaning they spend more time at sea than their cousins.

Puffins are partial to herring, smelt, sand eels, and capelin, a fish that feeds on zooplankton along the edges of Arctic ice shelves.

most dives last 20 to 30 seconds at depths of no more than 20 feet (6.1 m). Puffins' eyes face slightly upward, which allows them to see fish moving around and above them. Their powerful wings help them maneuver quickly among dense **shoals** of fish that rapidly shift direction.

Although puffins will eat **crustaceans**, octopuses, squid, marine worms, and a variety of **zooplankton**, they are specialized for capturing small fish. Typically, puffins feed on fish from one to three inches (2.5–7.6 cm) long, but large puffins have been known to take fish up to seven inches (17.8 cm) long. Puffins have rasp-like tongues, similar to those of cats, and small, backward-facing spines on the roof of the mouth. When a puffin catches a fish, it presses its tongue up to snag the fish on these spines. In addition, a flexible hinge connects the lower part of the bill to the skull and allows the mouth to open. This hinge, which turns bright yellow during breeding season, is called a rosette. Such features allow a puffin to open its mouth wider to catch more fish while preventing other prey from escaping. Puffins typically catch about 10 fish at a time in this way, but when collecting food for offspring, puffins can carry as many as 70 fish back to shore.

Unrelated to true eels, sand eels are a favorite fish prey of puffins and are found in sandy seabeds.

Laughing gulls frequent coastal Canada in summertime, where they attempt to steal food from nesting puffins.

LOAFERS, PARENTS, AND PUFFLINGS

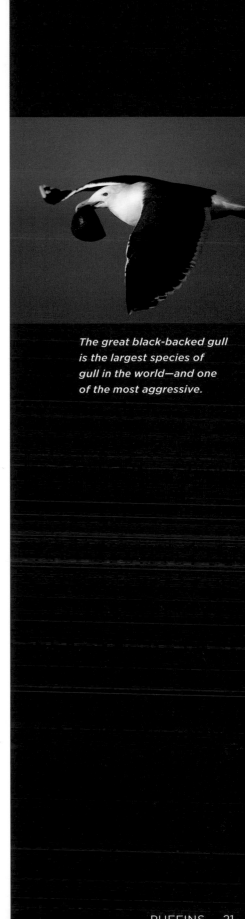

P uffins are highly social birds during spring and summer, but their behavior during the winter is a mystery to scientists. **Ornithologists** do know that they **migrate** both north and south, and they appear to spend their time far from land in the open ocean. Their predators include large fish, such as cod, monkfish, and sharks, as well as larger seabirds. The puffin's most deadly enemy is the great black-backed gull. With wingspans of five and a half feet (1.7 m), these birds snatch puffins from the air to eat them. Other types of gulls and auks linger around puffins and attack them— not to kill them, but to rob them. The larger birds peck the puffins' heads to get the puffins to drop their fish, which are then nabbed by the assailing birds.

When puffins are not feeding, they are usually preening. This is a form of grooming that keeps feathers waterproofed and in good shape. Feathers have tiny hooks called barbules that fit together. The barbules must be hooked together to provide the bird with **insulation**. Puffins use their bills to pull waxy oil from a **gland** near the tail and spread it over their feathers. This oil

The great black-backed gull is the largest species of gull in the world—and one of the most aggressive.

Vocalization is one strategy employed by puffins to warn intruders away from a nest.

Unlike most squawking, screeching seabirds, puffins are relatively quiet, making only low grumbles and barks.

waterproofs the feathers and keeps the barbules soft so that they remain tightly hooked together.

Unlike most birds their size, puffins are long-lived. They can survive up to 25 years in the wild and even longer in captivity. Puffins are old enough to reproduce by age three or four, but they typically do not breed until they are five years old. The breeding season begins in March or early April. Puffins gather together on rocky shores and cliffs of a mainland or on islands—many of which are quite small and uninhabited by humans. Such environments are called colonies. For the first few days, puffins sit or walk around, figuring out who is who. These gatherings are called clubs, and the behavior of relaxing and preening together is called loafing. After several days of socializing, puffins disperse from the club and begin the business of raising families.

Puffins like space around their burrows and may fight to keep other puffins from settling too nearby. Male puffins at odds over nest sites may battle each other by first ruffling their feathers and spreading their wings to show their size. Then they open their mouths and hold their tongues straight out. They may emit a low barking

sound. Such warnings are meant to make the weaker puffin give up. But equally matched puffins may engage in a fight with wing-beating, biting, and growling. Puffins have been known to be so preoccupied with fighting that they tumble over cliffs together. Fights rarely result in serious injury, though, since one puffin almost always concedes.

Puffins mate with the same partner year after year. Females usually arrive on land later than males, though, so a waiting male may select a backup female in case his original mate never arrives. If she does show up, the

Atlantic puffins acquaint themselves with their neighbors before moving to grassy nesting areas.

Clacking bills is one form of puffin communication that may lead to bonded partnerships and offspring.

male will leave the temporary mate and return to the first one. If one partner dies, the other will choose a new mate the following year. With thousands of birds gathered together, finding each other can be a challenge. Puffins do not remain paired while at sea, and scientists are not entirely sure how they recognize each other on land after eight months apart. Reunited puffins greet each other by nuzzling their heads and necks. They clack their bills together and nibble on each other's rosettes. Many puffin pairs return to a previously used nest site—an underground burrow, a ledge under a rock outcropping, or crevices among boulders. The male and female puffin share the task of digging out a burrow using their claws and bills. Then they gather soft grass with their bills to line the nest.

After mating, the male guards his partner from other males that may try to sneak up and mate with her. In southern habitats, females lay eggs as early as April. Closer to the Arctic, where winters last longer, eggs may not be laid until June. The puffin lays a single creamy-white egg, which can be as much as 15 percent of her body weight. Both parents take turns **incubating** the egg. The feathers

Tucking the feet close to the tail when flying (or when swimming underwater) reduces resistance.

While other seabirds fly close to the water's surface, puffins typically fly about 30 feet (9.1 m) above the ocean waves.

When feeding new pufflings, parents put fish directly into the chicks' mouths; eventually, they drop it on the burrow floor.

of a parent bird's breast near the wings fall out, leaving bare skin that emits heat through blood vessels close to the skin's surface. These are called brood patches. When a puffin nestles an egg, it presses this brood patch over the egg to keep it warm.

On land, puffins as well as their eggs and chicks face a variety of threats, not just from larger birds but also from land-dwelling animals such as stoats, rats, and dogs—all of which were introduced by humans generations ago. If an egg is damaged or taken by a predator within two weeks of being laid, puffins may create a second egg. But if the egg or the chick is lost later in the season, the puffin pair cannot produce a new offspring until the following year.

After a six-week incubation period, the chick—called a puffling—hatches. It weighs a little more than one ounce (28.3 g). Its body is covered with fluffy down. The parents take turns catching fish for their offspring. Puffins do not chew their food—they swallow it whole. Puffin parents must adjust the size of the fish they catch as their puffling grows. In about five weeks, flight feathers have replaced most of the down on the puffling's body, and it emerges from the nest for the first time. It does not stray

far from home, for it will need another week or two to get used to its surroundings and be fed by its parents. Then, when it leaves the burrow for good on a dark July or August night, the young puffin will be on its own. The parent puffins return to sea until the following year. Their offspring will not return to land until it is ready to find its own mate and continue the cycle of life.

Puffins typically dig their burrows anywhere from three to five feet (0.6–1.5 m) into the ground.

Puffins are considered a national treasure in Iceland, where the celebrated birds provided food for the country's first settlers.

CELEBRATING PUFFINS

Díðrikur á Skarvanesi, a 19th-century bird painter from the Faroe Islands, included an Atlantic puffin (top left) among his seabirds.

Today, the puffin is an instantly recognizable bird, considered by many to be clownish and cute. But the puffin was not always so adored. In medieval Britain, puffins were met with suspicion. Seeing a puffin on its own was considered unlucky. People chased puffins away or killed them to avoid the bad luck believed to follow lone puffins. After seeing one, people believed they could be protected from a puffin's curse only by taking off their shirt and putting it back on inside out. But one area of Britain has a long tradition of respecting puffins because of the bird's role in the **mythology** of King Arthur, the legendary fifth-century leader of Britain. A common element of King Arthur's story is that, upon his death, he was transformed into a bird. Various stories make him a crow, a wren, or a chough, but in southwestern England's Cornwall, storytellers say King Arthur became a nath, which is a traditional name for the puffin. Rarely seen in Cornwall, puffins are still revered there as being endowed with the spirit of King Arthur.

Perhaps nowhere on the planet are puffins more deeply rooted in human tradition than in the **culture**

The Viking Leif Erikson sailed to North America 500 years before Christopher Columbus.

First-time breeders return to their own birthplace, digging burrows near the spot where they were hatched.

of Iceland. The first human inhabitants of Iceland were Vikings. These people—from what is today Denmark, Norway, and Sweden—were the first humans to travel across the seas to Iceland, Greenland, and Canada. The Vikings settled in Iceland in the late ninth century. What they found were rocky shores, rolling hills, and millions of puffins and other seabirds. As settlers cleared land for dairy cattle, puffins became a main source of food. Puffin meat was salted and dried (similar to jerky). Because early settlers saw that puffins could both fly in the sky and swim underwater, they were not sure if the animals were birds or fish. Religious leaders warned against eating puffins, since their true nature was unknown. Many people ignored the warning, though, because historians credit puffins with saving the lives of many settlers who surely would have perished without the birds to sustain them.

Icelanders have never forgotten the importance of puffins to their heritage, and today, the birds are considered a national treasure. Sixty percent of the world's Atlantic puffin population nests in Iceland. People travel from around the world to see them. Boats carry tourists by the thousands every year to

visit puffin colonies. And puffins play a major role in Verslunarmannahelgi, Iceland's version of North America's Labor Day holiday. Celebrated the first Monday in August as well as the entire weekend before, this holiday features festivals, sports, music, and lots of puffins—particularly those served on a plate.

Even though Icelanders treasure their puffins, they still hunt them and make them part of holiday feasts. One of the biggest festivals, called Thjodhatid (*thoth-ha-TEETH*), occurs on Heimaey. This is the largest island of the Vestmannaeyjar (*VAHST-mahn-ah-AY-ish*) archipelago (also known as the Westman Islands, where 1.3 million

Scientists are not sure how breeding puffins manage to find their way back to their original nest sites.

FROM CHAPTER III

I still retain the most vivid impressions on my visit to the grand colony of Puffins on Doon, one of the St. Kilda group. Every available place is honeycombed with their holes; the ground cannot afford accommodation for all, and numbers of birds have to seek nesting places under the masses of rock lying on the grass-covered hillsides, or in the crannies of the cliffs at the summit of the island. As soon as we had fairly got ashore, and begun to walk up the slopes, the Puffins, in a dense whirling bewildering host, swept downwards to the sea, or rose high in the air to circle above our heads, in the direst alarm. It seemed as if the whole face of the island were slipping away from under me, just like flakes of shale down a quarry side! Not a single bird, so far as I could ascertain, uttered a note, but the whirring noise of the millions of rapidly beating wings sounded like the distant rush of wind! But even Doon does not harbour so many Puffins as find a home on the face of the mighty cliff Connacher; and when we fired a gun and disturbed them from this noble precipice, it seemed as though the face of the entire cliff was falling outwards into the Atlantic, the enormous cloud of birds overpowering one with its magnificence! As soon as the young are reared the land is deserted, and the wandering pelagic life resumed.

excerpt from British Sea Birds, *by Charles Dixon (1858–1926)*

puffins gather annually). A highlight of the festival is the preparation and serving of puffin, called *lundi* in Icelandic. Puffin meat is typically soaked in salt water, milk, or beer, and then browned in fat and smoked or grilled. Sometimes it is served with a blueberry sauce. Puffin reportedly tastes like duck with a fishy flavor.

In other parts of the world, where puffins are not nearly as abundant, the birds are equally loved. The Atlantic puffin is the official bird of Newfoundland and Labrador. Buddy the Puffin first appeared in 1992 as the mascot for the American Hockey League's St. John's Maple Leafs and remained the mascot when Newfoundland and Labrador's team became the IceCaps. Though a flag adopted by Newfoundland and Labrador in 1980 is meant to symbolize British heritage and a sword of honor, many people think it resembles a puffin's profile, with its mouth open and sharp tongue protruding.

Fictional puffins have been portrayed as clever birds. In the animated 3D movie *Happy Feet Two* (2011), the Mighty Sven is a puffin who flies away from a storm but continues south to escape being eaten first by polar bears and then humans on a research vessel. Sven ends up

Salt glands above a puffin's eyes and nostrils collect salt consumed while fishing, which the puffin gets rid of by shaking its head.

In 1996, the Atlantic puffin was included in a set of Canadian stamps called *Birds of Canada*.

Overhunting completely wiped out puffins in Maine, but Project Puffin helped the birds recolonize Eastern Egg Rock in 1981 and Seal Island in 1992.

among penguins in Antarctica, where he makes friends and enjoys his new home. Lieutenant Puffin first appeared in the 1994 animated movie *The Swan Princess*. He helped the princess Odette escape from a dungeon. Since then, he has appeared in a number of Swan Princess sequels.

Puffins have been no less successful on television. Hans the Puffin was a recurring character on *The Penguins of Madagascar*, an animated series that premiered on Nickelodeon in 2008 and ran for three seasons. Hans appears in several episodes, including "Huffin & Puffin," in which he hatches a plan to take control of the penguins' home. His failure results in his being sent to the Hoboken Zoo. Later, in the episode "The Hoboken Surprise," Hans helps his penguin neighbors defeat robotic animals trying to take over the zoo. The animated series *Puffin Rock* launched in 2015 in Great Britain and was made available in the United States on Netflix. The show is set on an island off the Irish coast. Viewers follow the adventures of a young puffin named Oona and her little brother, Baba, as they explore their world.

Many nations believe that puffins should be celebrated, so images of puffins have adorned postage stamps around

the world. St. Pierre and Miquelon, a French island collective off the coast of Newfoundland, issued a stamp in 2002 depicting Atlantic puffins taking flight from a cliff behind a puffin carrying fish in its bill. In 2013, the U.S. issued an 86-cent tufted puffin stamp. Three years later, Canada released a commemorative sheet of five stamps featuring birds of Canada. Among them was an Atlantic puffin in flight. Puffins have such worldwide appeal that even Malawi released a collection of bird stamps that included an Atlantic puffin in 2012, and the Republic of Guinea released a four-stamp set of waterfowl that included the tufted puffin in 2015.

The penguins in the movie Happy Feet Two *idolize an Atlantic puffin called the Mighty Sven for his ability to fly.*

Tufted puffins often gather during stormy weather to watch for small fish trapped close to shore by strong currents.

CHALLENGES AT SEA AND ON LAND

Puffins and their auk relatives all **evolved** from a common ancestor that existed in North America about 35 million years ago. Birds more closely resembling the modern puffin emerged about 15 million years ago. Fossils of several birds in the genus *Miocepphus* were discovered both in Maryland and California, suggesting that early puffins traveled either across the Arctic or the Isthmus of Panama (which was underwater) to reach both sides of North America. A flightless puffin relative inhabited coastal California and Mexico until about 470,000 years ago, and a fourth puffin species, the Dow's puffin, existed around California's Channel Islands through the end of the last glacial period, about 12,000 years ago. Scientists are not sure why Dow's puffins died out.

Today, more than half of the world's 10 to 12 million Atlantic puffins breed in Iceland. In North America, the highest concentration of Atlantic puffins is found in Newfoundland and Labrador, with about 500,000 breeding pairs. About 80 percent of the world's 3 million tufted puffins breed in and around Alaska. The largest colony in the continental U.S.—about 7,800 breeding

Natural preening oil reacts with sunlight to create vitamin D, which contributes to puffin health.

A genetic mutation called leucism can cause puffins to be nearly or completely white, though the bill and feet are still colorful.

pairs—is located on Jagged Island, off the coast of Washington. The entire world population of horned puffins is just over one million. About 85 percent of them nest in and around Alaska.

Puffins are not considered at risk in Iceland. However, in 2015, the International Union for Conservation of Nature (IUCN) listed Atlantic puffins as a vulnerable species because of a recent rapid decline in their numbers. The horned puffin appears on British Columbia's Red List of threatened species. In the U.S., the state of Maine has listed the Atlantic puffin as a threatened species, and in 2014, the Natural Resources Defense Council petitioned the U.S. Fish and Wildlife Service to add the tufted puffin to the U.S. Endangered Species List.

Scientists studying puffins believe that a number of factors are affecting puffin survival, including overfishing, pollution, invasive species, and human-influenced **climate change**. Fish oil, a form of Omega-3 fatty acid, is sold around the world as a dietary supplement. To meet the demand for this product, commercial fisheries take millions of small fish from puffin habitats, leaving a less than adequate supply of food for the birds. Pollution is

also a problem for puffins. In 2016, more than 10,500 gallons (39,747 l) of diesel fuel spilled from a factory in Northern Ireland, polluting a wildlife area where a rare group of 60 Atlantic puffins was being studied.

Plastic pollution is hazardous to puffins. A nurdle is a plastic ball about the size of a pea. Nurdles are made in factories and then shipped around the world to be made into virtually everything that can be constructed from plastic, from cups to computer cases. Nurdles often spill from trucks, trains, and ships, with millions of them ending up in the oceans. Because puffins eat small, floating sea creatures called copepods, they often ingest

Spreading its wings and stomping its feet are the first visible signs that a puffin is angry.

Puffins are among the estimated 90 percent of all bird species that form pair bonds during breeding season.

nurdles by mistake. Scientists studying Atlantic puffins on the Scottish Isle of May were the first to report instances of puffins having died from eating the plastic material.

Even light pollution causes trouble for puffins. Young puffins ready to leave their nests look to the sky at night for the moon and stars to guide them to sea. On nights when the moon is small or covered by clouds, puffins are instinctively drawn to the lights of towns. Instead of flying out to sea, they end up trapped in urban areas. Volunteers with organizations such as the Puffin & Petrel Patrol of Newfoundland and Labrador's Witless Bay area go out every night from August to October to rescue young puffins. The group works with the Canadian Wildlife Service (CWS) to weigh and measure each bird and put a numbered band on its leg. This helps the CWS monitor the health and breeding of returning puffins year after year.

On Destruction Island, off the coast of Washington, tufted puffins are being driven from their traditional nesting sites by nonnative rabbits. Not only do the rabbits deter puffins from nesting, they also devour the dense grass necessary to keep the burrows from collapsing on top of the puffins. A 2011 study by the Washington Department of Fish and Wildlife indicated that the breeding rate of tufted puffins on the island had dropped by 50 percent from previous years because of the growing rabbit population. Similarly, on Scotland's island of Craigleith, puffin nesting has decreased significantly because of an introduced plant: the tree mallow. This dense plant grows nearly 10 feet (3 m) tall and fills in puffin burrows, preventing the birds from laying eggs. Volunteers work to cut the plants each year, but getting rid of the plant without destroying other wildlife on the island is virtually impossible.

Among the many challenges facing puffins, perhaps none is more widespread and critical than human-

Unlike the burrow-digging Atlantic and tufted puffins, horned puffins typically nest in rock crevices and cliffs.

influenced climate change. Vast numbers of all three puffin species are turning up dead, washing ashore by the hundreds, while thousands more die at sea. The culprit, say researchers, is warming ocean temperatures that have thrown vital **food chains** out of whack and left entire populations of puffins starving to death.

Research conducted on the Bering Sea by the National Oceanic and Atmospheric Administration (NOAA) in 2016 found that warmer water temperatures have led to a mass die-off of the nutrient-rich copepods and other zooplankton that form the foundation of the ocean's food chain. Smaller fish and crustaceans feed on the copepods,

and marine animals feed on the fish and crustaceans. From puffins to sea lions to whales, animals on every level of the food chain have been dying by the thousands because of rising ocean temperatures.

Puffins are beloved birds that are facing a number of new challenges. They need to **adapt** quickly if they are to survive. Organizations such as Audubon's Project Puffin conduct research geared toward puffin conservation. But much more research on the effects of climate change and human interference with ocean **ecosystems** is vital if we are to protect Earth's puffin populations for generations to come.

Puffins typically need to get a running start to take off and often require a "runway" for landing as well.

ANIMAL TALE: THE GOLDEN-HAIRED PUFFIN

The Aleut people have inhabited the cold Aleutian Islands in the Bering Sea and western Alaska for thousands of years. Their traditions are rooted in a strong bond with wildlife, including puffins. This Aleut legend explains why the tufted puffin has golden "hair" during the summer months.

One day, the Aleut people wanted to dig for clams on a neighboring island. They waited until low tide. Then they got in their kayaks and paddled through the frigid sea. On the other island, the clams were plentiful. The people gathered as many as their kayaks could hold.

The tide began to rise, so the people headed for home. Suddenly, a dark cloud exploded overhead. A roaring wind came down from the sky, and the waves grew immense. The people were nearly back to their island when a heavy breaker came in from the sea. It rolled over the kayaks, tossing the people into the sea. Even with their protective *kamleika*—waterproof coats made of sea otter guts—they began to feel their blood turn to ice.

From his rocky island nearby, the puffin chief saw what was happening. He immediately gathered his clan, and they flew to rescue the people. The puffins dove into the water, plucked the people from death's grip, and carried them to shore. When all the people were safely back on their island, the Aleut chief was so grateful that he promised to reward the puffins with anything they desired.

Puffins have always been modest creatures. They have no need for anything except fish. The puffin chief was about to decline the offer when he spied the daughter of the people's chief. She had golden hair that was different from that of every other human the puffin chief had ever seen. He immediately fell in love with her and asked that she become his wife. With a heavy heart, the people's chief agreed, for he had made a promise.

The puffin chief welcomed his human wife to the rocky island of the puffins. He wanted to make her happy and comfortable in her new home, so he filled a cave with the skins of seals, sea otters, and Arctic foxes. Every day, he presented her with the most delicious fish, and every night, he wrapped himself in her long, golden hair and sang to her.

All summer, the puffin chief's wife seemed content, for she never complained. But the puffin chief often caught her looking sadly across the icy waves toward her family's island. She was an obedient wife, but she most certainly was not truly happy. This broke the puffin chief's heart. He loved his wife and wanted to spend the rest of his life with her. But, because he loved her, he could not bear to see her so sad.

So the puffin chief returned his wife to her people. She was grateful to the puffin chief and wanted to give him something to always remind him of their summer together. So she cut off her golden hair and wrapped it around the puffin chief's head. Then she bid him farewell as he flew back to his own island. And that is why, to this day, the tufted puffin wears golden tufts of hairlike feathers on his head.

GLOSSARY

adapt – change to improve its chances of survival in its environment

climate change – the gradual increase in Earth's temperature that causes changes in the planet's atmosphere, environments, and long-term weather conditions

crustaceans – animals with no backbone that have a shell covering a soft body

culture – a particular group in a society that shares behaviors and characteristics that are accepted as normal by that group

down – small feathers whose barbs do not interlock to form a flat surface, thus giving a fluffy appearance

ecosystems – communities of organisms that live together in environments

evolved – gradually developed into a new form

food chains – systems in nature in which living things are dependent on each other for food

gland – an organ in a human or animal body that produces chemical substances used by other parts of the body

incubating – keeping an egg warm and protected until it is time for it to hatch

insulation – the state of being protected from the loss of heat

keratin – a substance made of threadlike structures, the same substance that is found in human fingernails

migrate – to undertake a regular, seasonal journey from one place to another and then back again

mythology – a collection of myths, or popular, traditional beliefs or stories that explain how something came to be or that are associated with a person or object

ornithologists – scientists who study birds and their lives

plumage – the entire feathery covering of a bird

shoals – large groups of fish that are tightly condensed and moving as a single unit

tendon – a tough, inelastic tissue that connects muscle to bone

zooplankton – tiny sea creatures (some microscopic) and the eggs and larvae of larger animals

SELECTED BIBLIOGRAPHY

Dunn, Euan. *Puffins*. London: Bloomsbury, 2014.

"Horned Puffin." All About Birds – Cornell Lab of Ornithology. https://www.allaboutbirds.org/guide/Horned_Puffin/id.

Kaufman, Kenn. "Atlantic Puffin." Audubon. http://www.audubon.org/field-guide/bird/atlantic-puffin.

"Puffin FAQs." Audubon Project Puffin. http://projectpuffin.audubon.org/birds/puffin-faqs.

Sisson, Mark, and Dominic Couzens. *The Secret Lives of Puffins*. London: Bloomsbury, 2013.

Stirling, Katie. "*Fratercula cirrhata* – Tufted Puffin." Animal Diversity Web. http://animaldiversity.org/accounts/Fratercula_cirrhata/.

Note: Every effort has been made to ensure that any websites listed above were active at the time of publication. However, because of the nature of the Internet, it is impossible to guarantee that these sites will remain active indefinitely or that their contents will not be altered.

Puffins are sturdy little birds, but they are also fragile in many ways, as they depend on a balanced environment for survival.

INDEX